First Facts™

From Farm to Table

From Maple Trees to Maple Syrup

by Kristin Thoennes Keller

Consultant:
Tom McCrumm, Executive Director
Massachusetts Maple Producers Association
Ashfield, Massachusetts

Capstone *press*

Mankato, Minnesota

First Facts is published by Capstone Press
151 Good Counsel Drive, P.O. Box 669, Mankato, Minnesota 56002
www.capstonepress.com

Library of Congress Cataloging-in-Publication Data
Thoennes Keller, Kristin.
    From maple trees to maple syrup / by Kristin Thoennes Keller.
    p. cm.—(First facts. From farm to table)
    Includes bibliographical references (p. 23) and index.
    ISBN 0-7368-2634-3 (hardcover)
    1. Maple syrup—Juvenile literature. 2. Maple—Juvenile literature. [1. Maple syrup. 2. Maple.]
I. Title. II. Series.
TP395.T48 2005
641.3'364—dc22   2003023371

Summary: An introduction to the basic concepts of food production, distribution, and consumption
    by tracing the production of maple syrup from maple trees to the finished product.

Editorial Credits
Roberta Schmidt, editor; Jennifer Bergstrom, designer; Kelly Garvin, photo researcher; Eric Kudalis,
    product planning editor

Photo Credits
Capstone Press/Gary Sundermeyer, front cover (pancakes), 5 (foreground), 19
Fulton's Pancake House & Sugar Bush/Lorraine Downey, 15
Grant Heilman Photography/Larry Lefever, 16–17
Lynn M. Stone, 6–7, 8–9
PhotoDisc Inc., front cover (leaves), back cover, 1
Richard Hamilton Smith Photography/Blue Lake Studios LLC/Richard Hamilton Smith, 11,
    12–13, 14
Visuals Unlimited/John Sohldon, 10
Woolwich Observer/Elmira, ON, Canada, 20

Artistic Effects
PhotoDisc Inc., 5 (background)

1 2 3 4 5 6 09 08 07 06 05 04

Table of Contents

Sweet Maple Syrup

Maple syrup is a sweet treat. Many people eat maple syrup on waffles or pancakes. Maple syrup sometimes is used to make cakes, cookies, and candy.

Maple syrup has to be made before people can eat it. Making maple syrup takes many steps.

Fun Fact!
Maple syrup is made only in the United States and Canada.

Syrup Starts with Sap

Maple syrup is made from the **sap** of sugar maple trees. Sap is a liquid inside trees. Sap moves a tree's food up and down the trunk. Healthy trees make a lot of sap. People can take some of the sap without hurting the trees. They can use it to make maple syrup.

Maple Orchards

A group of sugar maple trees is called a **maple orchard** or sugarbush. The trees must grow for many years before a **sugarmaker** can take the sap. The sap begins to move, or run, inside the trees in early spring. The sugarmaker gathers the sap before the trees start to get leaves.

 Fun Fact!
A healthy sugar maple tree can live more than 200 years.

9

Gathering Sap

The sugarmaker **drills** a hole into the tree. A tap is put into the hole. Sap drips from the tap into a bucket. Full buckets are emptied into tanks.

Some sugarmakers use hoses to gather sap. One end of the hose is attached to the tap. The sap flows through the hose from the tree to a tank.

Boiling Sap

The sap is moved from tanks to a nearby building. This building is called a **sugar shack** or sugarhouse. The sap is put in a large pan over a fire. The sap is heated until it boils. Water in the sap turns into steam. The sap becomes thicker and sweeter as the water boils away.

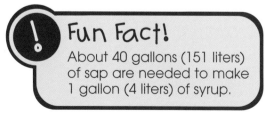

Fun Fact!
About 40 gallons (151 liters) of sap are needed to make 1 gallon (4 liters) of syrup.

13

Filtering Syrup

The sap boils until it becomes syrup. The sugarmaker tests the sap. The sap turns into syrup when it is at least two-thirds sugar.

Next, the syrup goes through a **filter**. Filters often are made of paper or cloth. The filter makes the syrup clean and pure.

To the Store

After the syrup passes through the filter, it is ready to be sold. The syrup is poured into metal cans, plastic jugs, or glass bottles. Some sugarmakers sell their syrup to stores. Trucks, trains, and airplanes take the syrup to the stores.

Where to Find Maple Syrup

Maple syrup can be found in many places. Grocery stores, restaurants, and bakeries sell maple syrup. Many sugarmakers sell their maple syrup at their maple orchards. No matter where people buy it, maple syrup is one of nature's sweet treats.

Fun Fact!
Most pancake syrup has little or no maple syrup in it. Pancake syrup is mostly corn syrup.

Amazing but True!

Elmira, Ontario, in Canada is the home of one of the largest maple syrup festivals in the world. The Elmira Maple Syrup Festival has been going on every year since 1965. In 2000, more than 80,000 people visited the festival. They ate 180 gallons (681 liters) of maple syrup on 15,000 servings of pancakes.

Hands On: Sugar-on-Snow

Sugar-on-snow is a treat in areas that make maple syrup. Ask an adult to help you make sugar-on-snow. This recipe uses ice instead of snow.

What You Need

1 quart (1 liter) of pure maple syrup
¼ teaspoon (1.2 mL) butter
3-quart (3-liter) saucepan
spoon
candy thermometer
finely crushed ice
flat pan or shallow bowl
fork

What You Do

1. Heat the maple syrup and butter in a saucepan on the stove. Stir the syrup to keep it from burning.
2. Use a candy thermometer to check the temperature of the syrup. Boil the syrup until it reaches 232°F (111°C).
3. Remove the saucepan from the stove. Let the syrup cool.
4. While the syrup is cooling, put some ice into a flat pan or shallow bowl.
5. Slowly pour the hot, thick syrup onto the ice. The syrup will get chewy, like taffy. When it cools, scoop up the syrup with a fork and eat it.

Glossary

drill (DRIL)—to make a hole

filter (FIL-tur)—something that takes out unwanted materials

maple orchard (MAY-puhl OR-churd)—a group of sugar maple trees; maple orchards also are called sugarbushes.

sap (SAP)—the liquid that flows through a plant; sap carries water and food from one part of the plant to another.

sugarmaker (SHUG-ur-mayk-ur)—a farmer who turns maple tree sap into maple syrup

sugar shack (SHUG-ur SHAK)—the building where sap is boiled to make maple syrup; sugar shacks also are called sugarhouses.

Read More

Mitchell, Melanie. *From Maple Tree to Syrup.* Start to Finish. Minneapolis: Lerner, 2004.

Schwartz, David M. *Maple Tree.* A Springboards into Science Series. Milwaukee: Gareth Stevens, 2001.

Stone, Lynn M. *Maple Syrup.* Harvest to Home. Vero Beach, Fla.: Rourke, 2002.

Internet Sites

FactHound offers a safe, fun way to find Internet sites related to this book. All of the sites on FactHound have been researched by our staff.

Here's how:
1. Visit *www.facthound.com*
2. Type in this special code **0736826343** for age-appropriate sites. Or enter a search word related to this book for a more general search.
3. Click on the **Fetch It** button.

FactHound will fetch the best sites for you!

Index